D0553792

Seeing God's Heart When You Hurt

TEXT AND PAINTINGS BY

Sandy Lynam Clough

HARVEST HOUSE PUBLISHERS
Eugene, Oregon

Seeing God's Heart When You Hurt

Text Copyright © 2001 by Sandy Lynam Clough
Published by Harvest House Publishers
Eugene, OR 97402

Library of Congress Cataloging-in-Publication Data

Clough, Sandy Lynam, 1948-
    Seeing God's heart when you hurt / text and paintings by Sandy Lynam Clough.
        p. cm.
    ISBN 0-7369-0519-7
    1. Suffering—Religious aspects—Christianity. I. Title.

    BV4909 .C58 2001
    242'.4—dc21

                                                    00-061403

Design and production by Garborg Design Works, Minneapolis, Minnesota

Unless indicated otherwise, verses are from The Amplified Bible. Old Testament copyright © 1965, 1987 by the Zondervan Corporation. The Amplified New Testament copyright © 1954, 1958, 1987 by the Lockman Foundation. Used by permission. Verses marked NAS are from the New American Standard Bible, © 1960, 1962, 1963, 1968, 1971, 1972, 1975, 1977 by The Lockman Foundation. Used by permission. Verses marked TLB are from The Living Bible, copyright © 1971. Used by permission of Tyndale House Publishers, Inc., Wheaton, Illinois 60189. All rights reserved.

Printed in Hong Kong.

01 02 03 04 05 06 07 08 09 10 /NG/ 10 9 8 7 6 5 4 3 2 1

Dedication

To our wonderful Lord,

who not only loves us and

watches us carefully but also

makes it possible for us

to see His heart

Contents

There Is More! 6

On the Inside 8

He Hears Me 14

He Helps Me 18

For Him 26

How Wonderful He Is! 32

The Greatest Gift 36

To my hurting friends...

There Is More!

*I*know what it is like to have a problem that never gets better, a physical need that has not been healed, and an emotional nightmare of fear. I'm writing to you because the Lord walked me out of that nightmare. Actually, He showed me a way out of it that may be a way for you, too—even if your circumstances never get better, either.

Looking in His Word for what He was telling about Himself healed my heart so deeply, that the nightmare faded away, leaving me with peace, joy, and a real confidence in Him and His personal care for my life—

even though my circumstances have never improved. The Lord is ready to do that for you, too! But wait! There's more! As time has given me perspective, I see that my months of suffering actually were the chance of a lifetime because I had an opportunity simply too wonderful to miss and I want to share that with you.

We're going to look for God's loving heart in this book. As you begin to "see" it, I'm sure He will do something wonderful in your heart. Perhaps for the first time in your life, you will know how to do something just for Him! Don't give up—the best is yet to come.

Sandy Lynam Clough

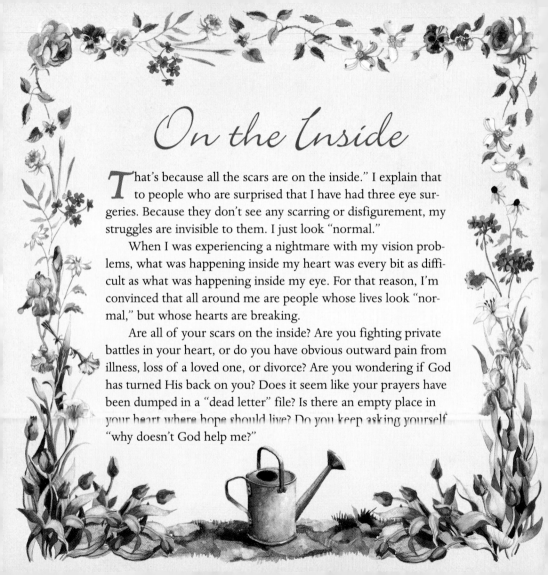

On the Inside

"That's because all the scars are on the inside." I explain that to people who are surprised that I have had three eye surgeries. Because they don't see any scarring or disfigurement, my struggles are invisible to them. I just look "normal."

When I was experiencing a nightmare with my vision problems, what was happening inside my heart was every bit as difficult as what was happening inside my eye. For that reason, I'm convinced that all around me are people whose lives look "normal," but whose hearts are breaking.

Are all of your scars on the inside? Are you fighting private battles in your heart, or do you have obvious outward pain from illness, loss of a loved one, or divorce? Are you wondering if God has turned His back on you? Does it seem like your prayers have been dumped in a "dead letter" file? Is there an empty place in your heart where hope should live? Do you keep asking yourself "why doesn't God help me?"

Perhaps because all your pain is on the inside, you feel it's apparent to no one but you. But there is One who sees—not only sees but also watches you very carefully. He is the same One who said to the man with the withered hand, "Stretch out your hand." He already knew what the man's hand looked like, but He asked him to stretch it forth before He healed the man.

Don't be afraid to say, "Lord, this is where it hurts." Show Him your withered hopes and your hurting heart. Trace His heart within His words, and then let Him show you His heart that has the power to heal all that is withered within you.

I found out for myself that sometimes it is hard to see Him while I am looking anxiously about in my circumstances. Even before I was able to see His obvious care in my circumstances, I knew without a doubt that He was watching me when I started watching Him back! He describes Himself in His Word so I can have a place to look. A place where I can be certain I'll see Him.

There are Scriptures that give voice to your pain. No matter what the source of that hurt is, together we can look for His heart in His Word and find not only comfort but also an opportunity. These pleas for help can be your own…

I entreated Thy favor with all my heart; be gracious to me according to Thy word.

PSALM 119:58 NAS

My soul weeps because of grief; strengthen me according to Thy word.

PSALM 119:28 NAS

Be to me a rock of refuge in which to dwell, and a sheltering stronghold to which I may continually resort, which You have appointed to save me, for You are my Rock and my Fortress.

PSALM 71:3

Remember the word to Thy servant, in which Thou hast made me hope. This is my comfort in my affliction, that Thy word has revived me.

PSALM 119:49, 50 NAS

In the day of on You, for

I am exceedingly afflicted; revive me, O LORD, according to Thy word.

PSALM 119:107 NAS

Deal with Thy servant according to Thy lovingkindness, and teach me Thy statutes.

PSALM 119:124 NAS

O may Thy lovingkindness comfort me, according to Thy word to Thy servant.

PSALM 119:76 NAS

My eyes fail with longing for Thy word, while I say, "When wilt Thou comfort me?"

PSALM 119:82 NAS

Sustain me according to Thy word, that I may live; and do not let me be ashamed of my hope.

PSALM 119:116 NAS

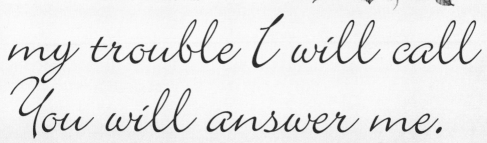

my trouble I will call You will answer me.

PSALM 86:7

Look upon my affliction for I do not forget

Hear my voice according to Thy lovingkindness; revive me, O LORD, according to Thine ordinances.

PSALM 119:149 NAS

Yes, You are my Rock and my Fortress; therefore for Your name's sake lead me and guide me.

PSALM 31:3

Establish my footsteps in Thy word, and do not let any iniquity have dominion over me.

PSALM 119:133 NAS

Rescue me out of the mire, and let me not sink; let me be delivered from those who hate me and from out of the deep waters. Let not the flood waters overflow and overwhelm me, neither let the deep swallow me up nor the [dug] pit [with water perhaps in the bottom] close its mouth over me.

PSALM 69:14,15

Keep and protect me, O God, for in You I have found refuge, and in You do I put my trust and hide myself.

PSALM 16:1

12

and rescue me, Thy law.

PSALM 119:153 NAS

Answer me, O LORD,
for Thy lovingkindness is
good; according to the
greatness of Thy
compassion, turn to me....

PSALM 69:16 NAS

My inner self
thirsts for God,
for the living God.
When shall I
come and behold
the face of God?

PSALM 42:2

I will say to God
my Rock, Why
have You forgotten
me? Why go I
mourning because of
the oppression
of the enemy?

PSALM 42:9

Sandy Lynam Clough

He Hears Me

One of the songs that has comforted and encouraged me the most says, "His eye is on the sparrow and I know He watches me." How do I *know* that He's watching me? In His Word, I watched Him back! I looked at what He says about Himself. He has described Himself in His Word so we can see exactly what He is like. Psalm 4:3 says that He hears me when I call to Him.

Knowing that He hears me gives me hope. His Word also tells me that He is watching and planning for me. Not only does He hear my cries, He also hears your pleas for help. These verses will assure you of that…

14

Blessed be God,
Who has not turned away
my prayer, nor His lovingkindness from me.

PSALM 66:20 NAS

Behold, the Lord's eye is upon those who fear Him [who revere and worship Him with awe], who wait for Him and hope in His mercy and loving–kindness.

PSALM 33:18

I will rejoice and be glad in Thy lovingkindness, because Thou hast seen my affliction; Thou hast known the troubles of my soul.

PSALM 31:7 NAS

O Thou who dost hear prayer,
to Thee all men come.

PSALM 65:2 NAS

The eyes of the LORD are toward the righteous, and His ears are
open to their cry.... The righteous cry and the LORD hears, and
delivers them out of all their troubles. The LORD is near to the
brokenhearted, and saves those who are crushed in spirit.

PSALM 34:15-18 NAS

15

I love the LORD, because He
hears my voice and my supplications.

PSALM 116:1 NAS

...He does not forget

He Who planted the
ear, shall He not hear?
He Who formed the
eye, shall He not see?

PSALM 94:9

*Because He has inclined
His ear to me, therefore
will I call upon Him as
long as I live.*

PSALM 116:2

16

The Lord has heard my supplication;
the Lord receives my prayer.

PSALM 6:9 NAS

the cry of the afflicted.

PSALM 9:12 NAS

To Him Who [earnestly] remembered us in our low estate and imprinted us [on His heart], for His mercy and loving-kindness endure forever.

PSALM 136:23

I will confess, praise, and give thanks to You, for You have heard and answered me; and You have become my Salvation and Deliverer.

PSALM 118:21

The Lord gazes down upon Mankind from heaven where he lives. He has made their hearts and closely watches everything they do.

PSALM 33:13-15 TLB

He Helps Me

*I*n the crisis I found myself in, I knew that if the Lord didn't help me, there would be no help for me. Because I could not yet see how He was working to help me, I was both afraid and frustrated. Have you ever asked, "Why doesn't He help me?" Take heart. The way the Lord describes Himself in His Word not only tells me that He hears me, He tells me how He will help me! As you "see" Him in these verses, look for the ways He is both willing and able to help you.

In peace I will both lie down and sleep, for You, Lord, alone make me dwell in safety and confident trust.

PSALM 4:8

The LORD is my light and my salvation; whom shall I fear? The LORD is the defense of my life; whom shall I dread?

PSALM 27:1 NAS

Show Your marvelous lovingkindness, O You Who save by Your right hand those who trust and take refuge in You from those who rise up against them.

PSALM 17:7

My defense and shield depend on God, Who saves the upright in heart.

PSALM 7:10

And those who know Thy name will put their trust in Thee; for Thou, O LORD, hast not forsaken those who seek Thee.

PSALM 9:10 NAS

The Lord also will be a refuge and a high tower for the oppressed, a refuge and a stronghold in times of trouble (high cost, destitution, and desperation).

PSALM 9:9

You are a hiding place for me; You, Lord, preserve me from trouble, You surround me with songs and shouts of deliverance.

PSALM 32:7

The LORD will give strength to His people; the LORD will bless His people with peace.

PSALM 29:11 NAS

Our inner selves wait [earnestly] for the Lord; He is our Help and our Shield.

PSALM 33:20

For with You is the fountain of life; in Your light do we see light.

PSALM 36:9

But the salvation of the [consistently] righteous is of the Lord; He is their Refuge and secure Stronghold in the time of trouble.

PSALM 37:39

God is our refuge a very present help

Thou, O LORD, wilt not withhold Thy compassion from me; Thy lovingkindness and Thy truth will continually preserve me.

PSALM 40:11 NAS

My God in His lovingkindness will meet me....

PSALM 59:10A NAS

We have thought of your steadfast love, O God....

PSALM 48:9A

Why are you cast down, O my inner self? And why should you moan over me and be disquieted within me? Hope in God and wait expectantly for Him, for I shall yet praise Him, Who is the help of my countenance, and my God.

PSALM 42:11

and strength, in trouble.

PSALM 46:1 NAS

Nevertheless I am
You do hold

I will cry to God Most High, Who performs on my behalf and rewards me [Who brings to pass His purposes for me and surely completes them]!

PSALM 57:2

He only is my Rock and my Salvation; He is my Defense and my Fortress, I shall not be moved.

PSALM 62:6

God is to us a God of deliverances; and to GOD the Lord belong escapes from death.

PSALM 68:20 NAS

Bless the LORD, O my soul, and forget none of His benefits.

PSALM 103:2 NAS

continually with You; my right hand.

Blessed be the Lord, Who bears our burdens and carries us day by day, even the God Who is our salvation!

PSALM 68:19

If I should say, "My foot has slipped," Thy lovingkindness, O LORD, will hold me up.

PSALM 94:18 NAS

The Lord executes righteousness and justice [not for me only, but] for all who are oppressed.

PSALM 103:6

Who forgives [every one of] all your iniquities, Who heals [each one of] all your diseases....

PSALM 103:3

Behold, God is my helper and ally; the Lord is my upholder and is with them who uphold my life.

PSALM 54:4

O my strength, I will sing praises to Thee; for God is my stronghold, the God who shows me lovingkindness.

PSALM 59:17 NAS

23

For You have delivered my life from death, my eyes from tears, and my feet from stumbling and falling.

PSALM 116:8

As a father loves and pities his children, so the Lord loves and pities those who fear Him [with reverence, worship, and awe].

PSALM 103:13

He has sent redemption to His people; He has commanded His covenant to be forever; holy is His name, inspiring awe, reverence, and godly fear.

PSALM 111:9

He has given food and provision to those who reverently and worshipfully fear Him; He will remember His covenant forever and imprint it [on His mind].

PSALM 111:5

For He satisfies fills the

24

But there is forgiveness with You [just what man needs], that You may be reverently feared and worshiped.

PSALM 130:4

The LORD will accomplish what concerns me; Thy lovingkindness, O LORD, is everlasting; do not forsake the works of Thy hands.

PSALM 138:8 NAS

For this God is our God forever and ever; He will be our guide [even] until death.

PSALM 48:14

the longing soul and hungry soul with good.

PSALM 107:9

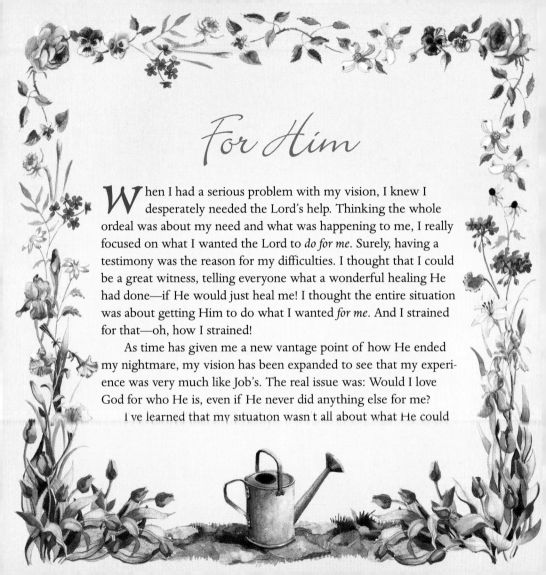

For Him

When I had a serious problem with my vision, I knew I desperately needed the Lord's help. Thinking the whole ordeal was about my need and what was happening to me, I really focused on what I wanted the Lord to *do for me*. Surely, having a testimony was the reason for my difficulties. I thought that I could be a great witness, telling everyone what a wonderful healing He had done—if He would just heal me! I thought the entire situation was about getting Him to do what I wanted *for me*. And I strained for that—oh, how I strained!

As time has given me a new vantage point of how He ended my nightmare, my vision has been expanded to see that my experience was very much like Job's. The real issue was: Would I love God for who He is, even if He never did anything else for me?

I've learned that my situation wasn't all about what He could do for me, it was my best opportunity to do something *for Him*. It was the chance of a lifetime to speak what He tells me is true of Himself in His Word in my darkest places. It was my opportunity to say, "Yes, my circumstances are dark, but have you noticed how He shines because He is the light." Corrie ten Boom's sister Betsie told Corrie that people would believe their testimony from a Nazi prison camp because "we were here." In my affliction, people give attention to my witness because of what I am experiencing. When I point out how wonderful He is, it is a more powerful witness because my life is not perfect.

The end of the book of Job tells us that God was pleased with Job because he had spoken what was right about Him. To offer sacrifice of praise in my darkest places is the opportunity of a lifetime to do something for my Lord as I call attention to His wonderful attributes. I can honor Him for His very heart when I cannot guess His hand. We all have the same opportunity that Job had when we hurt. Have you considered his story and how it demonstrates the privilege we have?

And the LORD said to Satan, "Have you considered My servant Job? For there is no one like him on the earth, a blameless and upright man, fearing God and turning away from evil." Then Satan answered the LORD, "Does Job fear God for nothing? Hast Thou not made a hedge about him and his house and all that he has, on every side? Thou hast blessed the work of his hands, and his possessions have increased in the land."

JOB 1:8-10 NAS

SATAN WAS SURE JOB
LOVED GOD BECAUSE HE
GAVE HIM LOTS OF STUFF.

"But put forth Thy hand now and touch all
that he has; he will surely curse Thee to
Thy face." Then the LORD said to Satan,
"Behold, all that he has is in your power,
only do not put forth your hand on him."
So Satan departed from the presence of the
LORD.

JOB 1:11,12 NAS

IN ONE DAY JOB
LOST HIS SONS,
HIS DAUGHTERS,
HIS OXEN, DONKEYS,
AND CAMELS
(HIS LIVELIHOOD),
AND HIS SERVANTS.

Then Job arose and tore his
robe and shaved his head,
and he fell to the ground and
worshiped. And he said,
"Naked I came from my
mother's womb, and
naked I shall return
there. The LORD gave
and the LORD has
taken away. Blessed be
the name of the LORD."
Through all this Job did not
sin nor did he blame God.

JOB 1:20-22 NAS

Sandy Lynam Clough

29

And the LORD said to Satan, "Have you considered My servant Job? For there is no one like him on the earth, a blameless and upright man fearing God and turning away from evil. And he still holds fast his integrity, although you incited Me against him, to ruin him without cause." And Satan answered the LORD and said, "Skin for skin! Yes, all that a man has he will give for his life. However, put forth Thy hand, now, and touch his bone and his flesh; he will curse Thee to Thy face."

…Then Satan went out from the presence of the LORD, and smote Job with sore boils from the sole of his foot to the crown of his head. And he took a potsherd to scrape himself while he was sitting among the ashes. Then his wife said to him, "Do you still hold fast your integrity? Curse God and die!" But he said to her, "You speak as one of the foolish women speaks. Shall we indeed accept good from God and not accept adversity?" In all this Job did not sin with his lips.

JOB 2:3-10 NAS

Sandy Lynam Clough

30

As Job's suffering came to an end, and right before God blessed him with twice as much as he had before, the Lord rebuked Job's friends for not saying what was right.

And it came about after the Lord had spoken these words to Job, that the Lord said to Eliphaz the Temanite, "My wrath is kindled against you and against your two friends, because you have not spoken of Me what is right as My servant Job has."

JOB 42:7 NAS

It is obvious that Satan wanted to prove that Job only loved God for what he could get out of Him. He never thought that Job might be willing to lay down his life rather than denounce God. Only Job could prove he loved God—for Himself. And he did—by saying what was true of God when his whole life was in shambles! We can do that too! We live in a world of people who do not love God for Himself. What a privilege we have to declare how worthy He is of our love!

How Wonderful He Is!

When I was tempted to question God's love and goodness in my most difficult days, I almost missed the most wonderful opportunity I've ever had—the opportunity to point out His goodness and His love in spite of my circumstances. Reading in His Word about all the ways in which He is wonderful brought me the gift of joy and confidence in Him. It is my joy to share it!

Have you begun to see His loving heart yet? Are you able to say, "Yes, my circumstances are bad, but have you noticed how wonderful He is?"

Here are some verses that can help you honor Him in hard places.

I Need Healing

Bless the LORD, O my soul; and forget none of his benefits; who pardons all your iniquities; who heals all your diseases; who redeems your life from the pit; who crowns you with lovingkindness and compassion....

PSALM 103:2–4 NAS

Nobody Loves Me

How precious is your steadfast love, O God! The children of men take refuge and put their trust under the shadow of Your wings.

PSALM 36:7

I Don't Know What's Going to Happen to Me

The counsel of the LORD stands forever, the plans of His heart from generation to generation.

PSALM 33:11 NAS

33

I Feel Like He's Forgotten Me

Can a woman forget her nursing child, and have no compassion on the son of her womb? Even these may forget, but I will not forget you. Behold, I have inscribed you on the palms of My hands....

ISAIAH 49:15,16B NAS

I Have Sinned

For Thou, O LORD, art good, and ready to forgive, and abundant in lovingkindness to all who call upon Thee.

PSALM 86:5 NAS

I Feel Like I'm Living in a Nightmare

When the righteous cry for help, the LORD hears and delivers them out of all their distress and troubles.

PSALM 34:17

I Have a Broken Heart

The LORD is near to the brokenhearted, and saves those who are crushed in spirit.

PSALM 34:18 NAS

I Have Sinned

For Thou, O LORD, art good, and ready to forgive, and abundant in lovingkindness to all who call upon Thee.

PSALM 86:5 NAS

I Am Alone

Blessed be God, who has not turned away my prayer, nor His lovingkindness from me.

PSALM 66:20 NAS

I Have Need

[As for me] I am poor and needy, yet the Lord takes thought and plans for me.

PSALM 40:17

The Greatest Gift

*I*n your weakest state, even if you feel like a failure, you may yet offer your greatest service to the Lord. When I am in difficulties, I can imagine that my heavenly Father sits a little closer to the edge of His throne and waits to hear what His child whom He loves so much will say about Him.

Saying what is true of my Lord when I am suffering is a gift of love and honor to Him. It also gives me the greatest gift I could ever have—a picture of His heart and the healing of mine. Scriptures that tell me the ways in which God is wonderful illumine my darkest days and help me see His heart.

Lord, You are wonderful because…

Salvation belongs to the Lord; May Your blessings be upon Your people.

PSALM 3:8

Great is the LORD and greatly to be praised....

PSALM 48:1 NAS

For You are not a God Who takes pleasure in wickedness; neither will the evil [man] so much as dwell [temporarily] with You.

PSALM 5:4

...the Lord is upright; He is my rock, and there is no unrighteousness in Him.

PSALM 92:15 NAS

Sandy Lynam Clough

For the LORD is righteousness; the upright

But as for me, I will enter Your house through the abundance of Your steadfast love and mercy; I will worship toward and at Your holy temple in reverent fear and awe of You.

PSALM 5:7

O Lord my God, in You I take refuge and put my trust; save me from all those who pursue and persecute me, and deliver me.

PSALM 7:1

Oh, let the wickedness of the wicked come to an end, but establish the [uncompromisingly] righteous [those upright and in harmony with You]; for You, Who try the hearts and emotions and thinking powers, are a righteous God.

PSALM 7:9

righteous; He loves
will behold His face.

PSALM 11:7 NAS

O Lord, our Lord,
how excellent
(majestic and
glorious) is Your
name in all the
earth! You have
set Your glory on
[or above]
the heavens.

PSALM 8:1

*But the Lord shall
remain and continue
forever; He has
prepared and
established His
throne for judgment.*

PSALM 9:7

*I will give to the Lord the thanks due to His
rightness and justice, and I will sing praise
to the name of the Lord Most High.*

PSALM 7:17

*I will praise You, O Lord, with my whole heart; I will show forth (recount
and tell aloud) all Your marvelous works and wonderful deeds!*

PSALM 9:1

39

*I say to the Lord, You are my Lord;
I have no good beside or beyond You.*

PSALM 16:2

The law of the Lord is perfect, restoring the [whole] person; the testimony of the Lord is sure, making wise the simple.

PSALM 19:7

As for God, His way is blameless; the word of the LORD is tried; He is a shield to all who take refuge in Him.

PSALM 18:30 NAS

But You are holy, O You Who dwell in [the holy place where] the praises of Israel [are offered].

PSALM 22:3

The Lord is my Rock, my Fortress, and my Deliverer; my God, my keen and firm Strength in Whom I will trust and take refuge, my Shield, and the Horn of my salvation, my High Tower.

PSALM 18:2

*The Heavens declare the glory of God; and the
firmament shows and proclaims His handiwork.*

PSALM 19:1

Sandy Lynam Clough
©1989

41

Let the words of my mouth and the meditation of my heart be acceptable in Your sight, O Lord, my [firm, impenetrable] Rock and my Redeemer.

PSALM 19:14

The voice of the Lord is powerful; the voice of the Lord is full of majesty.

PSALM 29:4

Remember, O LORD, Thy compassion and Thy lovingkindnesses, for they have been from of old.

PSALM 25:6 NAS

Ascribe to the LORD, O sons of the mighty, ascribe to the LORD glory and strength.

PSALM 29:1 NAS

...*You are my Strength*

For Thy lovingkindness is before my eyes, and I have walked in Thy truth.

PSALM 26:3 NAS

Oh, how great is Your goodness, which You have laid up for those who fear, revere, and worship You, goodness which You have wrought for those who trust and take refuge in You before the sons of men!

PSALM 31:19

To the end that my tongue and my heart and every-thing glorious within me may sing praise to You and not be silent. O Lord my God, I will give thanks to You forever.

PSALM 30:12

Good and upright is the LORD; therefore He instructs sinners in the way.

PSALM 25:8 NAS

You have redeemed me, O Lord, the God of truth and faithfulness.

PSALM 31:5

For the kingship and the kingdom are the Lord's, and He is the ruler over the nations.

PSALM 22:28

and my Stronghold.

PSALM 31:4B

O taste and see that the
blessed is the man who

For the word of the LORD is upright; and all His work is done in faithfulness. He loves righteousness and justice; the earth is full of the lovingkindness of the LORD.

PSALM 33:4,5 NAS

Let those who favor my righteous cause and have pleasure in my uprightness shout for joy and be glad and say continually, Let the Lord be magnified, Who takes pleasure in the prosperity of His servant.

PSALM 35:27

Why are you cast down, O my inner self? And why should you moan over me and be disquieted within me? Hope in God and wait expectantly for Him, for I shall yet praise Him, my Help and my God.

PSALM 42:5

LORD is good; how takes refuge in Him!

PSALM 34:8 NAS

"Cease striving and know that I am God; I will be exalted among the nations, I will be exalted in the earth."

PSALM 46:10 NAS

Many, O Lord my God, are the wonderful works which You have done, and Your thoughts toward us; no one can compare with You! If I should declare and speak of them, they are too many to be numbered.

PSALM 40:5

Thy lovingkindness, O LORD, extends to the heavens, Thy faithfulness reaches to the skies.

PSALM 36:5 NAS

And my tongue shall talk of Your righteousness, rightness, and justice, and of [my reasons for] Your praise all the day long.

PSALM 35:28

The Mighty One, God,
the Lord, speaks and calls
the earth from the rising
of the sun to its setting.

PSALM 50:1

Once God has spoken, twice I have
heard this: That power belongs to God....

PSALM 62:11 NAS

For God is the King of
all the earth; sing praises
in a skillful psalm and
with understanding.
God reigns over the
nations; God sits upon
His holy throne.

PSALM 47:7,8

For Thy lovingkindness
heavens, and Thy

The lovingkindness
of God endures all
day long.

PSALM 52:1B NAS

Great is the LORD, and greatly to
be praised, in the city of our
God, His holy mountain.

PSALM 48:1 NAS

He will send from heaven and save me; He reproaches him who tramples upon me. God will send forth His lovingkindness and His truth.

PSALM 57:3 NAS

But as for me, I shall sing of Thy strength; yes, I shall joyfully sing of Thy lovingkindness in the morning, for Thou hast been my stronghold, and a refuge in the day of my distress.

PSALM 59:16 NAS

is great to the truth to the clouds.

PSALM 57:10 NAS

O my Strength, I will watch and give heed to You and sing praises; for God is my Defense (my Protector and High Tower).

PSALM 59:9

47

Sandy Lynam Clough

You crown the year with your bounty and goodness....

PSALM 65:11A

O God, awe-inspiring, profoundly impressive, and terrible are You out of Your holy places; the God of Israel Himself gives strength and fullness of might to His people. Blessed be God!

PSALM 68:35

For You are my hope; O Lord God, You are my trust from my youth and the source of my confidence.

PSALM 71:5

Ascribe power and strength to God; His majesty is over Israel, and His strength and might are in the skies.

PSALM 68:34

He rules by His might forever, His eyes observe and keep watch over the nations; let not the rebellious exalt themselves.

PSALM 66:7

Upon You have I leaned and relied from birth; You are He Who took me from my mother's womb and You have been my benefactor from that day. My praise is continually of You.

PSALM 71:6

49

But He, full of [merciful] compassion, forgave their iniquity and destroyed them not; yes, many a time He turned His anger away and did not stir up all His wrath and indignation.

PSALM 78:38

My flesh and my heart may fail, but God is the Rock and firm Strength of my heart and my Portion forever.

PSALM 73:26

God blesses us, of the earth

With God rests my salvation and my glory; He is my Rock of unyielding strength and impenetrable hardness, and my refuge is in God!

PSALM 62:7

Surely God is good to Israel, to those who are pure in heart!

PSALM 73:1 NAS

You will guide me with Your counsel, and afterward receive me to honor and glory.

PSALM 73:24

That they may know that You,
Whose name alone is the Lord, are
the Most High over all the earth.

PSALM 83:18

You are the God Who does
wonders; You have demonstrated
Your power among the peoples.

PSALM 77:14

that all the ends
may fear Him.

PSALM 67:7 NAS

Sing aloud to God our
Strength! Shout for joy
to the God of Jacob!

PSALM 81:1

The day is Yours, the
night also is Yours; You
have established the
[starry] light and the sun.

PSALM 74:16

Sandy Lynam Clough

For the Lord God is a Sun and Shield; the Lord bestows [present] grace and favor and [future] glory (honor, splendor, and heavenly bliss)! No good thing will He withhold from those who walk uprightly. O Lord of hosts, blessed (happy, fortunate, to be envied) is the man who trusts in You, [leaning and believing on You, committing all and confidently looking to You, and that without fear or misgiving]!

PSALM 84:11,12

For Thou art wondrous deeds;

Yes, the Lord will give what is good,
and our land will yield its increase.
PSALM 85:12

For great is
Your mercy and
lovingkindness
toward me; and
You have delivered
me from the depths
of Sheol [from the
exceeding depths
of affliction].
PSALM 86:13

For Thou, LORD,
art good, and ready
to forgive, and
abundant in
lovingkindness
to all who call
upon Thee.
PSALM 86:5 NAS

I will give
thanks to Thee,
O Lord my
God, with all
my heart, and
will glorify Thy
name forever.
PSALM 86:12 NAS

I will sing of
the mercy and
lovingkindness
of the Lord
forever; with
my mouth will I
make known
Your faithfulness
from generation
to generation.
PSALM 89:1

But Thou, O Lord, art a God merciful and gracious, slow
to anger and abundant in lovingkindness and truth.
PSALM 86:15 NAS

great and doest
Thou alone art God.
PSALM 86:10 NAS

But You, Lord, are on

O satisfy us in the morning with Thy lovingkindness,
that we may sing for joy and be glad all our days.

PSALM 90:14 NAS

How great are Your doings, O Lord!
Your thoughts are very deep.

PSALM 92:5

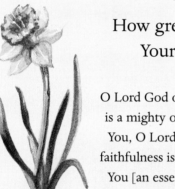

O Lord God of hosts, who is a mighty one like unto You, O Lord? And Your faithfulness is round about You [an essential part of You at all times]

PSALM 89:8

I will say of the Lord, He is my Refuge and my Fortress, my God; on Him I lean and rely, and in Him I [confidently] trust!

PSALM 91:2

Righteousness and justice are the foundation of your throne;
mercy and lovingkindness and truth go before Your face.

PSALM 89:14

high forever.

PSALM 92:8

...He is my rock, and there is no unrighteousness in Him.

PSALM 92:15B NAS

For the Lord is a great God, and a great King above all gods.

PSALM 95:3

For who in the heavens can be compared to the Lord? Who among the mighty [heavenly beings] can be likened to the Lord, a God greatly feared and revered in the council of the holy (angelic) ones, and to be feared and worshipfully revered above all those who are round about Him?

PSALM 89:6,7

But the Lord has become my High Tower and Defense, and my God the Rock of my refuge.

PSALM 94:22

Your throne is established from of old; You are from everlasting.

PSALM 93:2

For great is the Lord and greatly to be praised; He is to be reverently feared and worshiped above all [so-called] gods.

PSALM 96:4

...righteousness and justice are the foundation of His throne.

PSALM 97:2B

For You, Lord, are high above all the earth; You are exalted far above all gods.

PSALM 97:9

Honor and majesty are and beauty

O sing to the Lord a new song, for He has done marvelous things; His right hand and His holy arm have wrought salvation for Him.

PSALM 98:1

Say among the nations that the Lord reigns; the world also is established, so that it cannot be moved; He shall judge and rule the people righteously and with justice.

PSALM 96:10

Let them confess and praise
Your great name, awesome
and reverence inspiring! It
is holy, and holy is He!

PSALM 99:3

The Lord has made known His
salvation; His righteousness
has He openly shown in
the sight of the nations.

PSALM 98:2

*before Him; strength
are in His sanctuary.*

PSALM 96:6

For the Lord is good; His mercy and lovingkindness are
everlasting, His faithfulness and truth endure to all generations.

PSALM 100:5

But You, O Lord,
are enthroned forever;
and the fame of
Your name endures
to all generations.

PSALM 102:12

Extol the Lord our God and worship at His
holy hill, for the Lord our God is holy!

PSALM 99:9

I will sing of mercy and lovingkindness and
justice; to You, O Lord, will I sing.

PSALM 101:1

Bless (affectionately, gratefully praise) the Lord, O my soul! O Lord my God, You are very great! You are clothed with honor and majesty.

PSALM 104:1

For as the heavens are high above the earth, so great are His mercy and lovingkindness toward those who reverently and worship-fully fear Him.

PSALM 103:11

But the lovingkindness of the LORD is from everlasting to everlasting on those who fear Him, and His righteousness to children's children....

PSALM 103:17 NAS

O Lord, how many and varied are Your works! In wisdom have You made them all; the earth is full of Your riches and Your creatures.

PSALM 104:24

He will not always chide or be contending, neither will He keep His anger forever or hold a grudge.

PSALM 103:9

But Thou, O GOD, the Lord, deal kindly with me for Thy name's sake; because Thy lovingkindness is good, deliver me....

PSALM 109:21 NAS

The LORD is compassionate slow to anger and abounding in

Sing to Him, sing praises to Him; meditate on and talk of all His marvelous deeds and devoutly praise them.

PSALM 105:2

The works of the Lord are great, sought out by all those who have delight in them. His work is honorable and glorious, and His righteousness endures forever.

PSALM 111:2,3

Praise the LORD! Oh give thanks to the LORD, for He is good; for His lovingkindness is everlasting.

PSALM 106:1 NAS

For Your mercy and lovingkindness are great and high as the heavens! Your truth and faithfulness reach to the skies!

PSALM 108:4

and gracious, lovingkindness.

PSALM 103:8 NAS

59

The LORD is high above glory above

You who [reverently] fear the Lord, trust in and lean on the Lord! He is their Help and their Shield.

PSALM 115:11 NAS

Prosperity and welfare are in His house, and His righteousness endures forever.

PSALM 112:3

Sandy Lynam Clough

The works of His hands are [absolute] truth and justice [faithful and right]; and all His decrees and precepts are sure (fixed, established, and trustworthy)

PSALM 111:7

all nations, and His the heavens!

PSALM 113:4

Gracious is the Lord, and righteous; yes, our God is compassionate.

PSALM 116:5 NAS

Praise the LORD, all nations; laud Him, all peoples! For His lovingkindness is great toward us, and the truth of the LORD is everlasting. Praise the LORD!

PSALM 117 NAS

Let those now who reverently and worshipfully fear the Lord say that His mercy and lovingkindness endure forever.

PSALM 118:4

Not to us, O LORD, not to us, but to Thy name give glory because of Thy lovingkindness, because of Thy truth.

PSALM 115:1 NAS

The Lord is my Strength and Song; and He has become my Salvation.

PSALM 118:14

He has made His wonders to be remembered; the LORD is gracious and compassionate.

PSALM 111:4 NAS

Praise the Lord! (Hallelujah!) Praise the name of the Lord; praise Him, O you servants of the Lord!

PSALM 135:1

Let Your tender mercy and lovingkindness come to me that I may live, for Your law is my delight!

PSALM 119:77

Forever, O LORD, Thy word is settled in heaven.

PSALM 119:89 NAS

Thou art good teach me

I know, O Lord, that Your judgments are right and righteous, and that in faithfulness You have afflicted me.

PSALM 119:75

Give thanks to the LORD, for He is good; for His lovingkindness is everlasting.

PSALM 118:29 NAS

May those who fear Thee see me and be glad, because I wait for Thy word.

PSALM 119:74 NAS

The earth is full of Thy lovingkindness, O LORD; teach me Thy statutes.

PSALM 119:64 NAS

Give Thanks to the LORD, for He is good; for His lovingkindness is everlasting.

PSALM 136:1 NAS

According to Your steadfast love give life to me; then I will keep the testimony of Your mouth [hearing, receiving, loving, and obeying it].

PSALM 119:88

To Him Who alone does great wonders, for His mercy and lovingkindness endure forever.

PSALM 136:4

and doest good; Thy statutes.

PSALM 119:68 NAS

All Your commandments are faithful and sure. [The godless] pursue and persecute me with falsehood; help me [Lord]!

PSALM 119:86

Sandy Lynam Clough

They shall eagerly utter the memory of Thine abundant goodness, and shall shout joyfully of Thy righteousness.

PSALM 145:7 NAS

The LORD is gracious and merciful; slow to anger and great in lovingkindness.

PSALM 145:8 NAS

Thine eyes have seen my unformed substance; and in Thy book they were all written, the days that were ordained for me, when as yet there was not one of them.

PSALM 139:16 NAS

Your faithfulness is from generation to generation; You have established the earth, and it stands fast.

PSALM 119:90

For You cause my lamp to be lighted and to shine; the Lord my God illumines my darkness.

PSALM 18:28

64